KING OF THE SEA!

Sharks Coloring Book

JUPITER KIDS
CHILDREN'S & KIDS FICTION

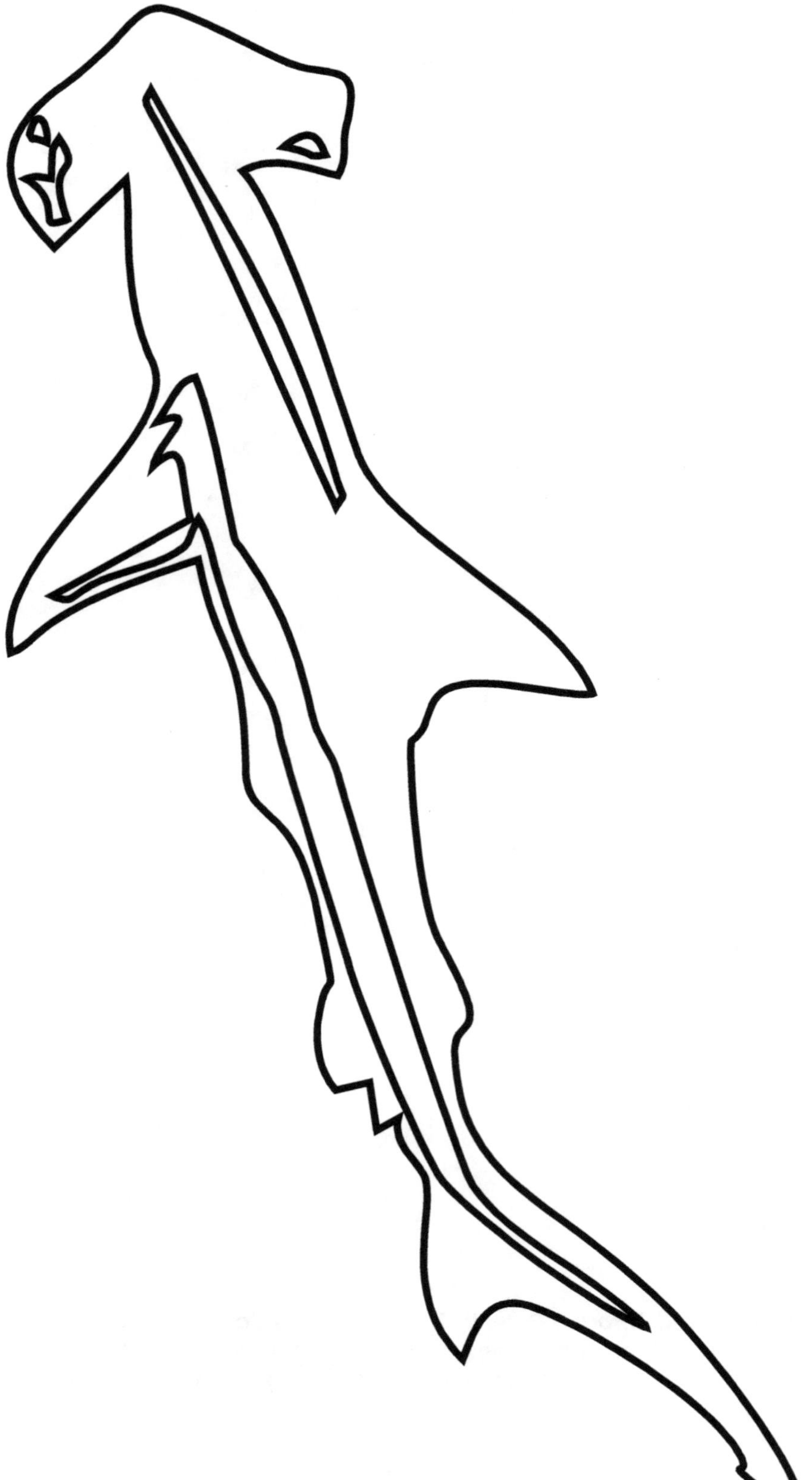

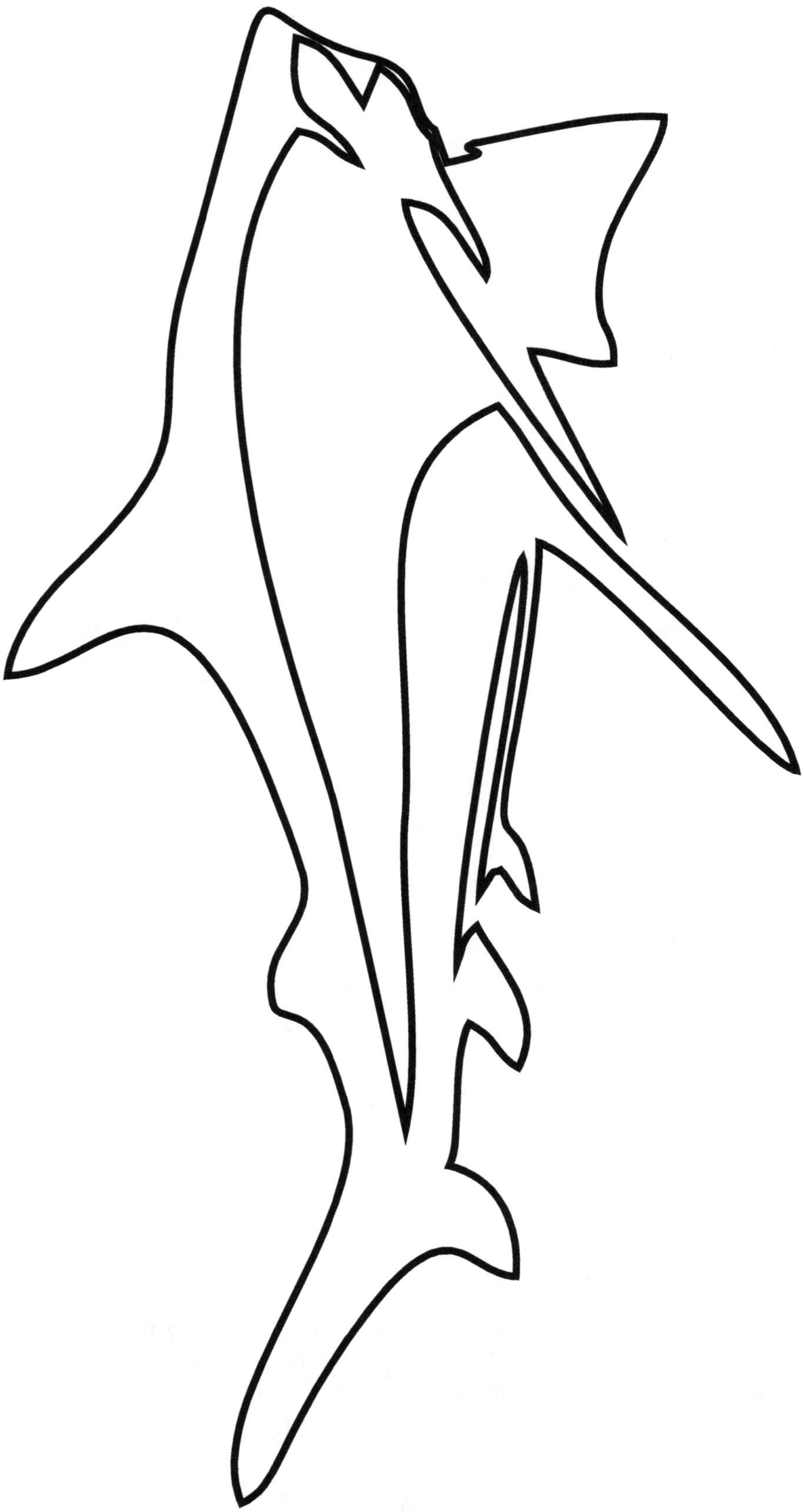

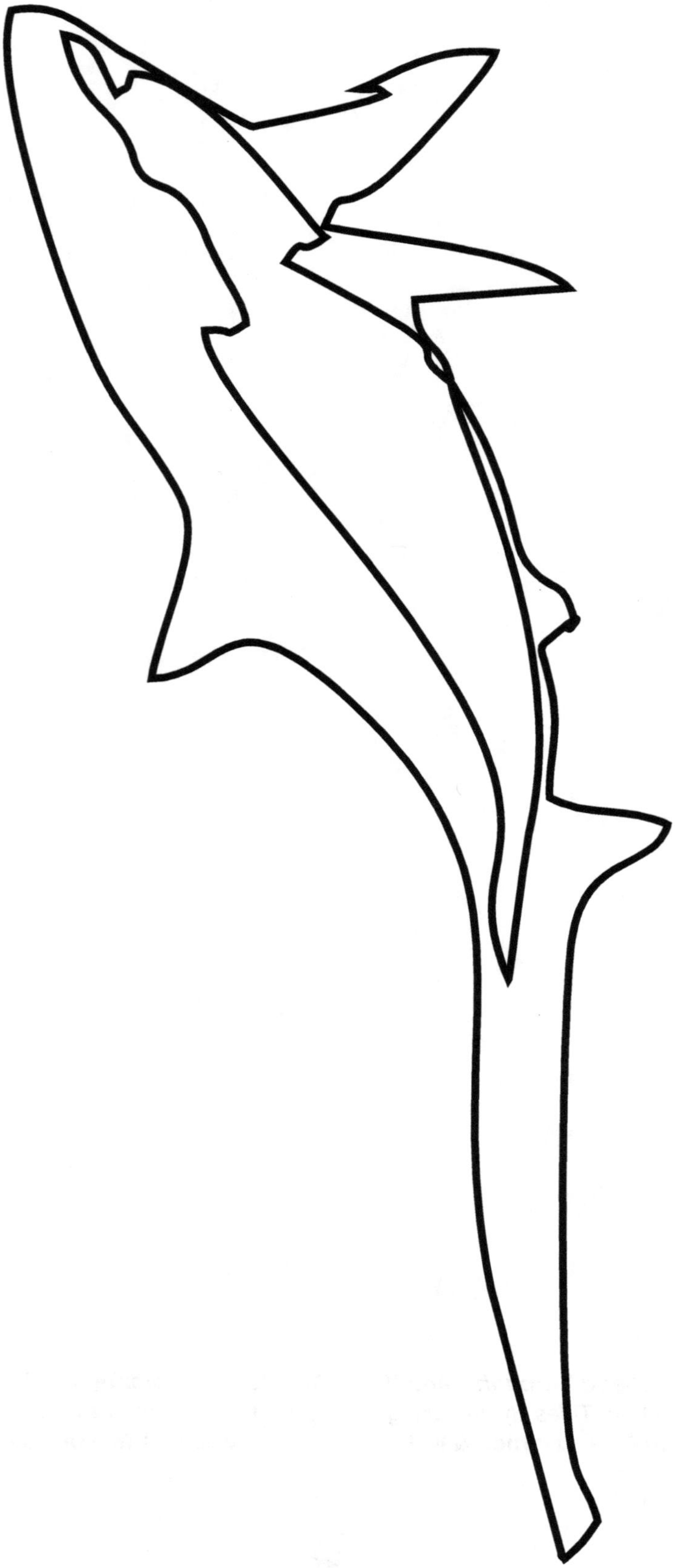

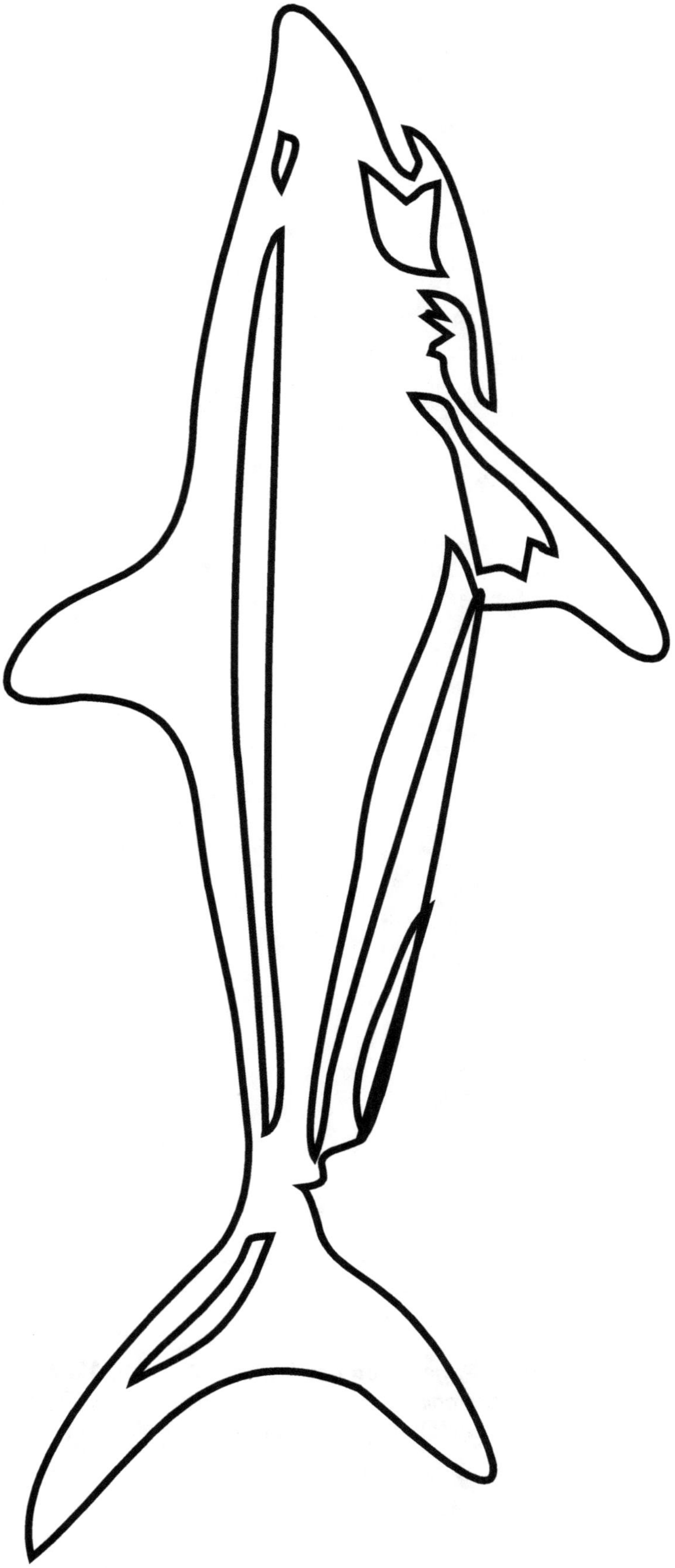

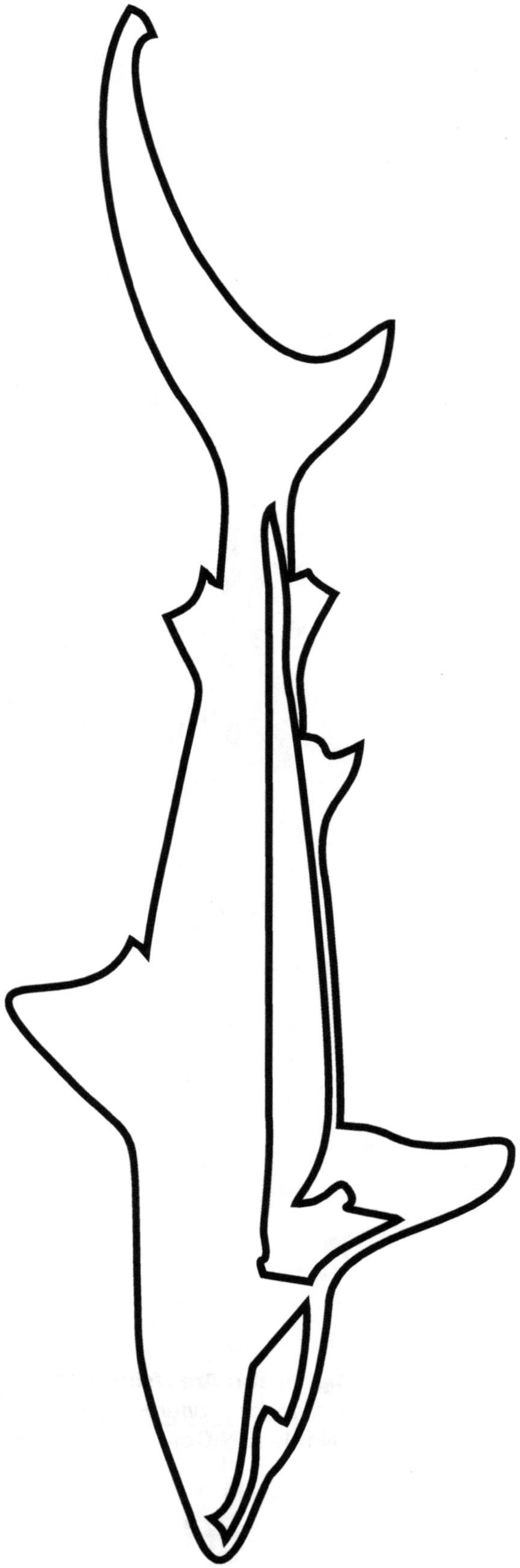

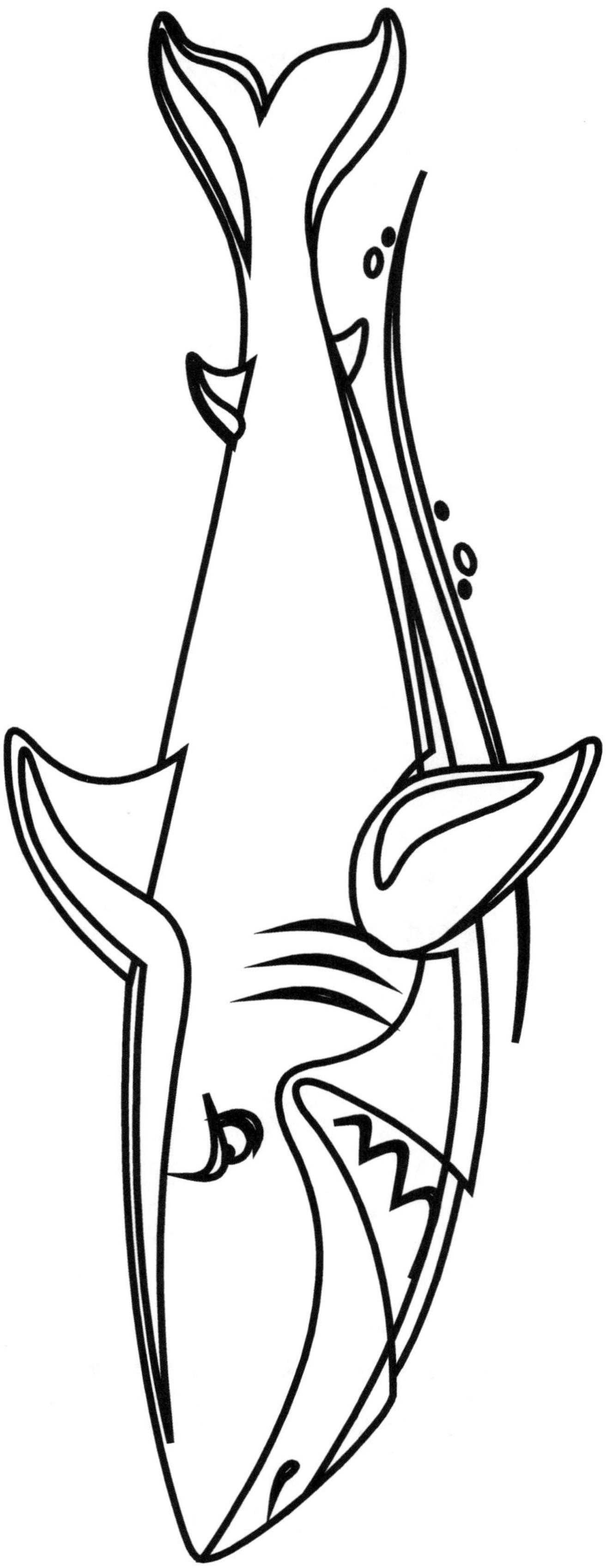

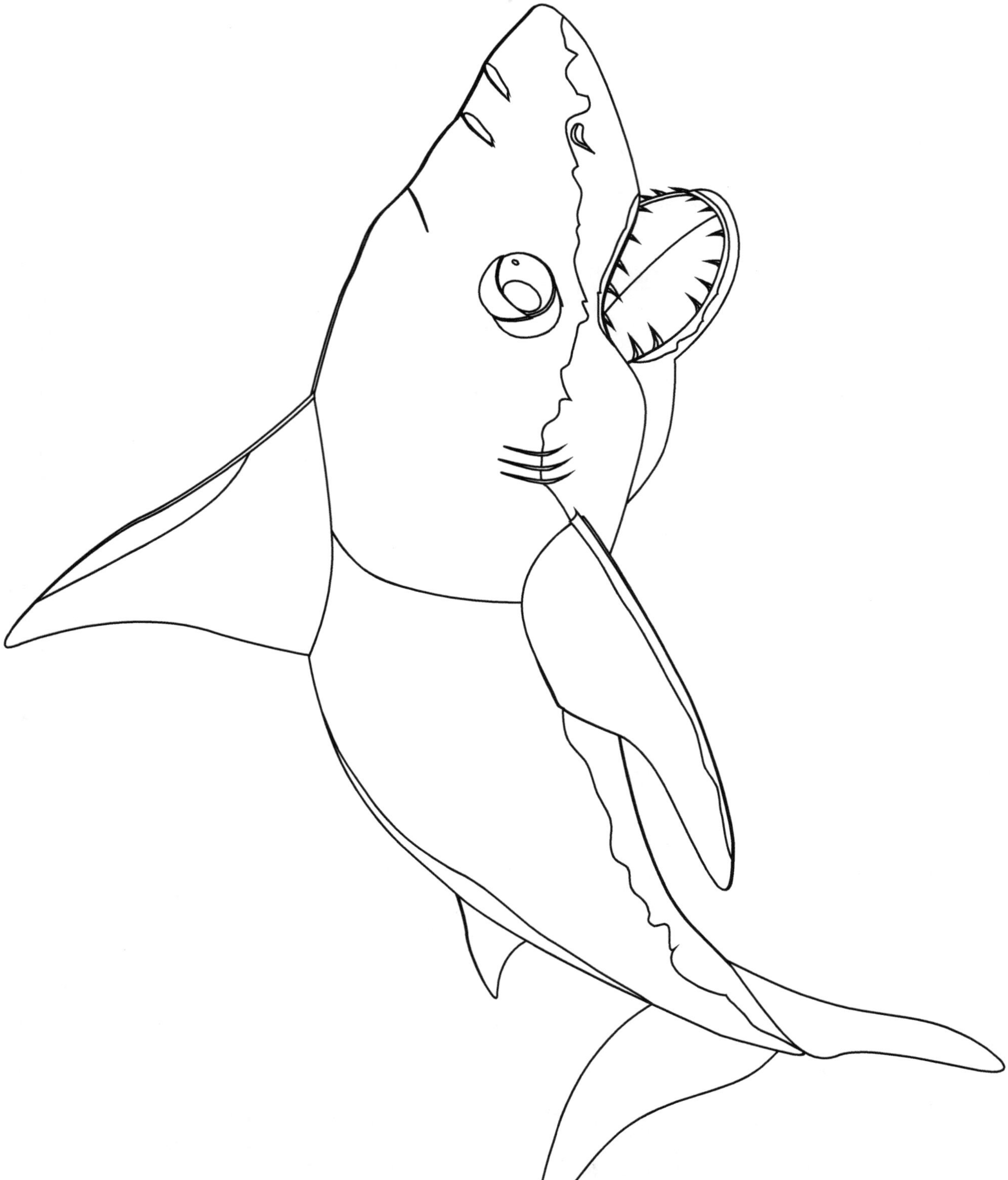

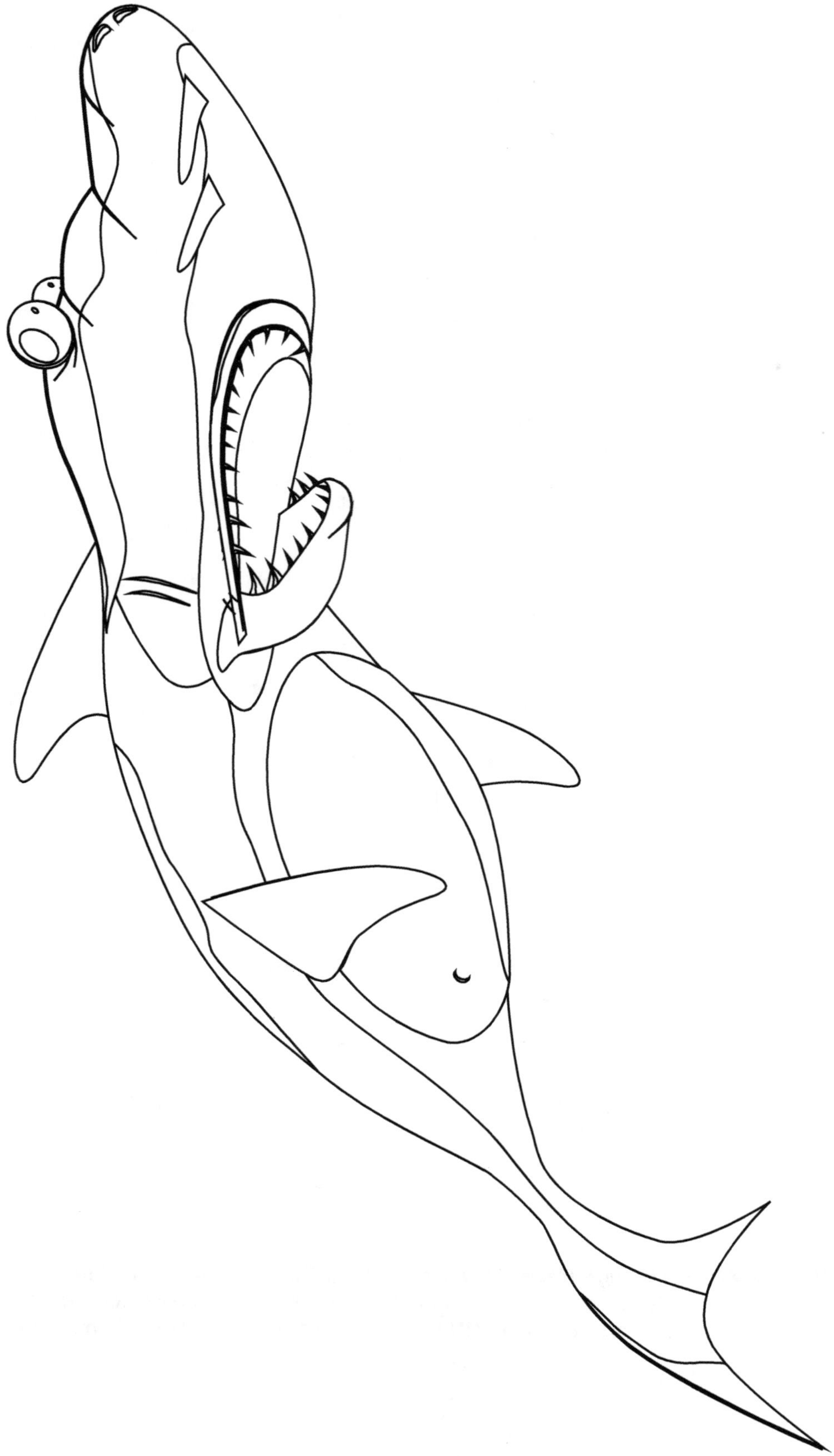

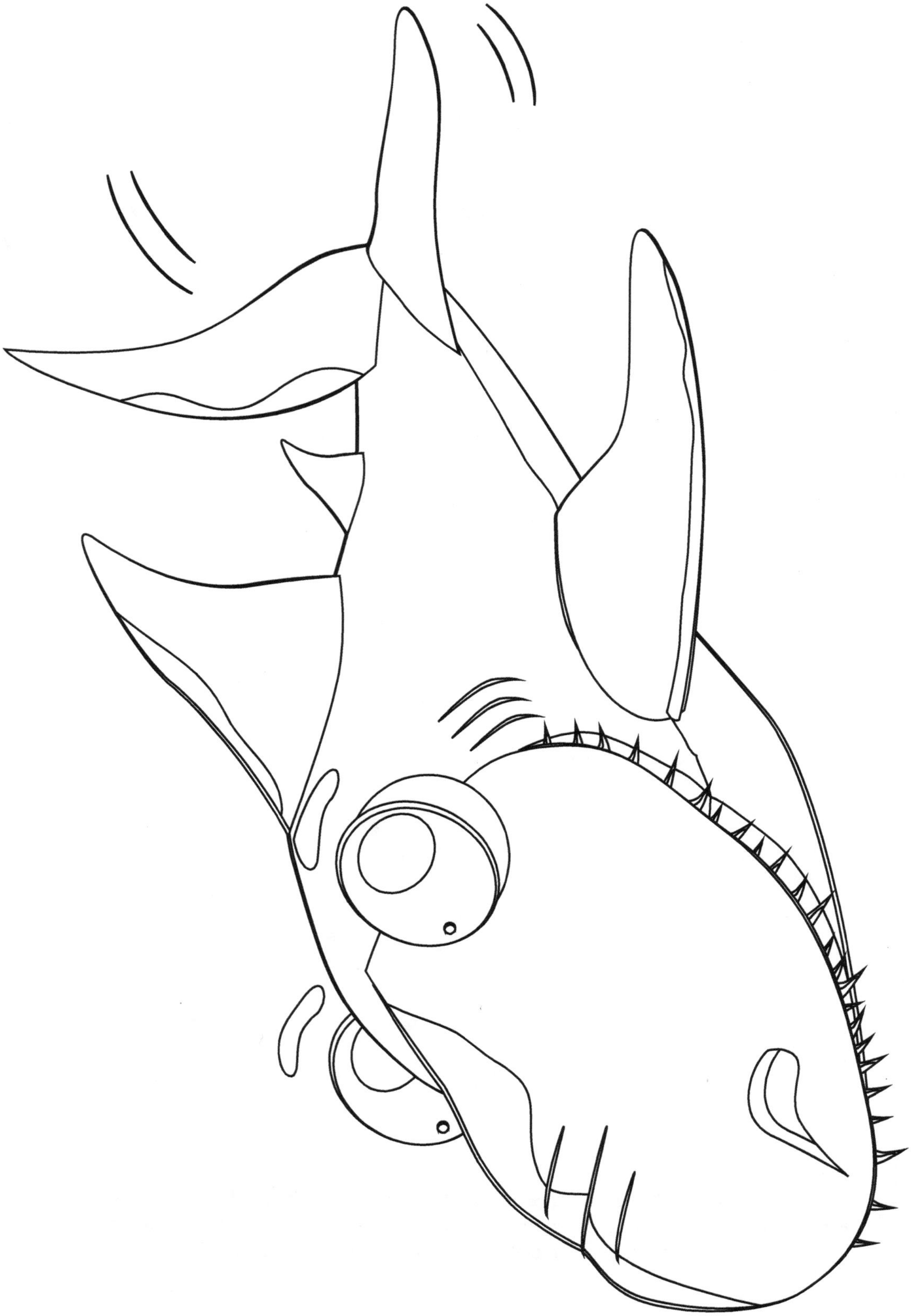

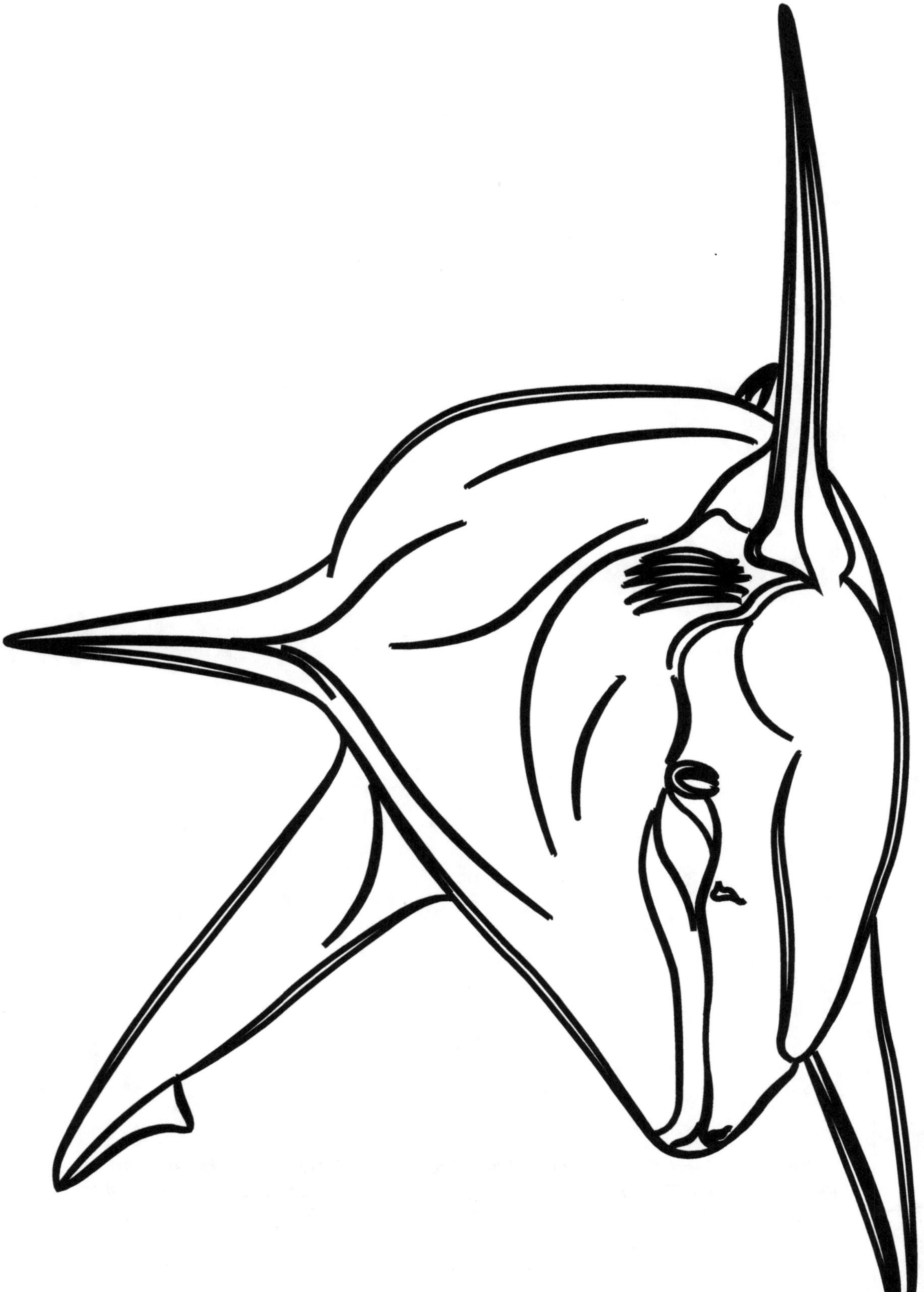

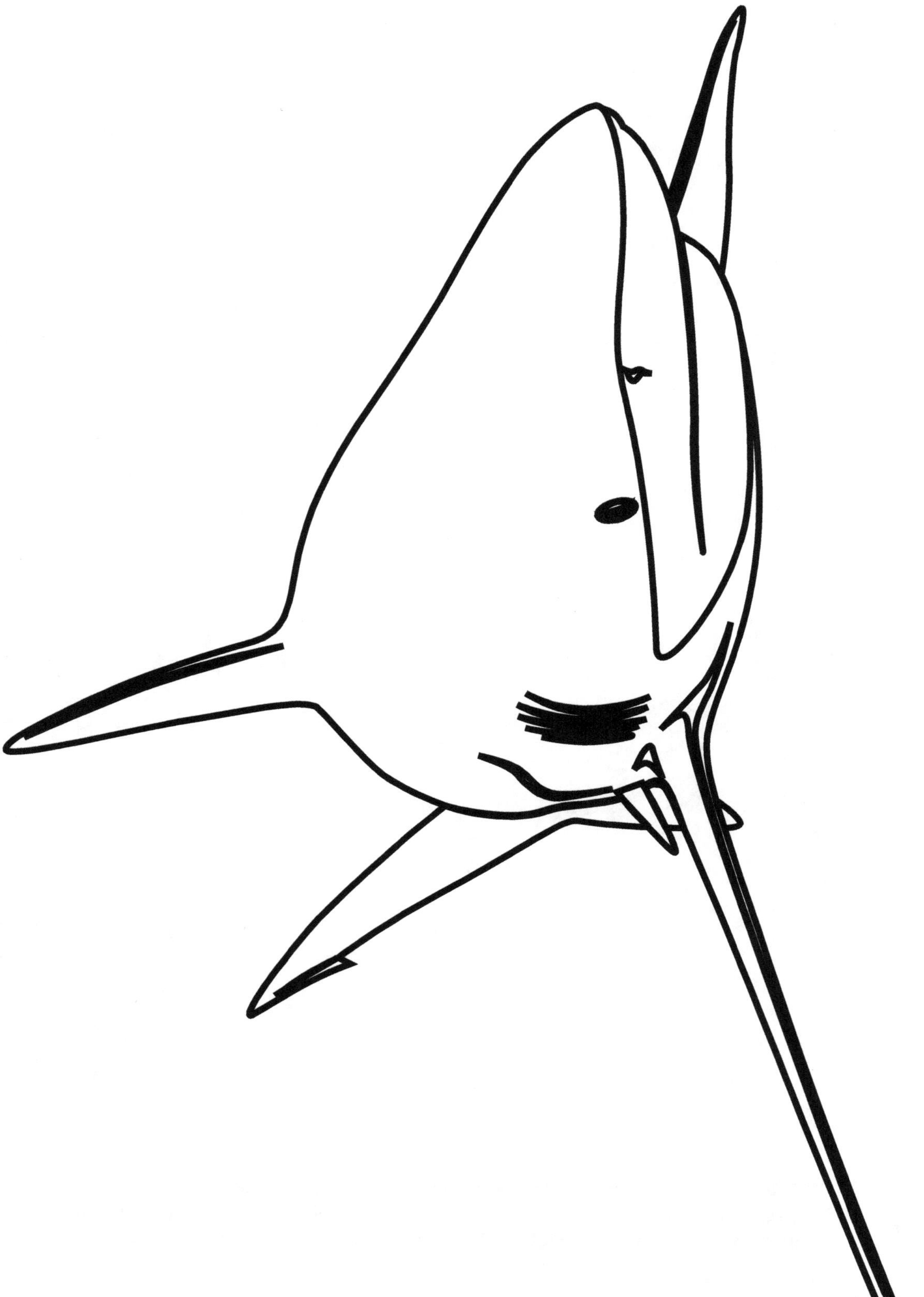

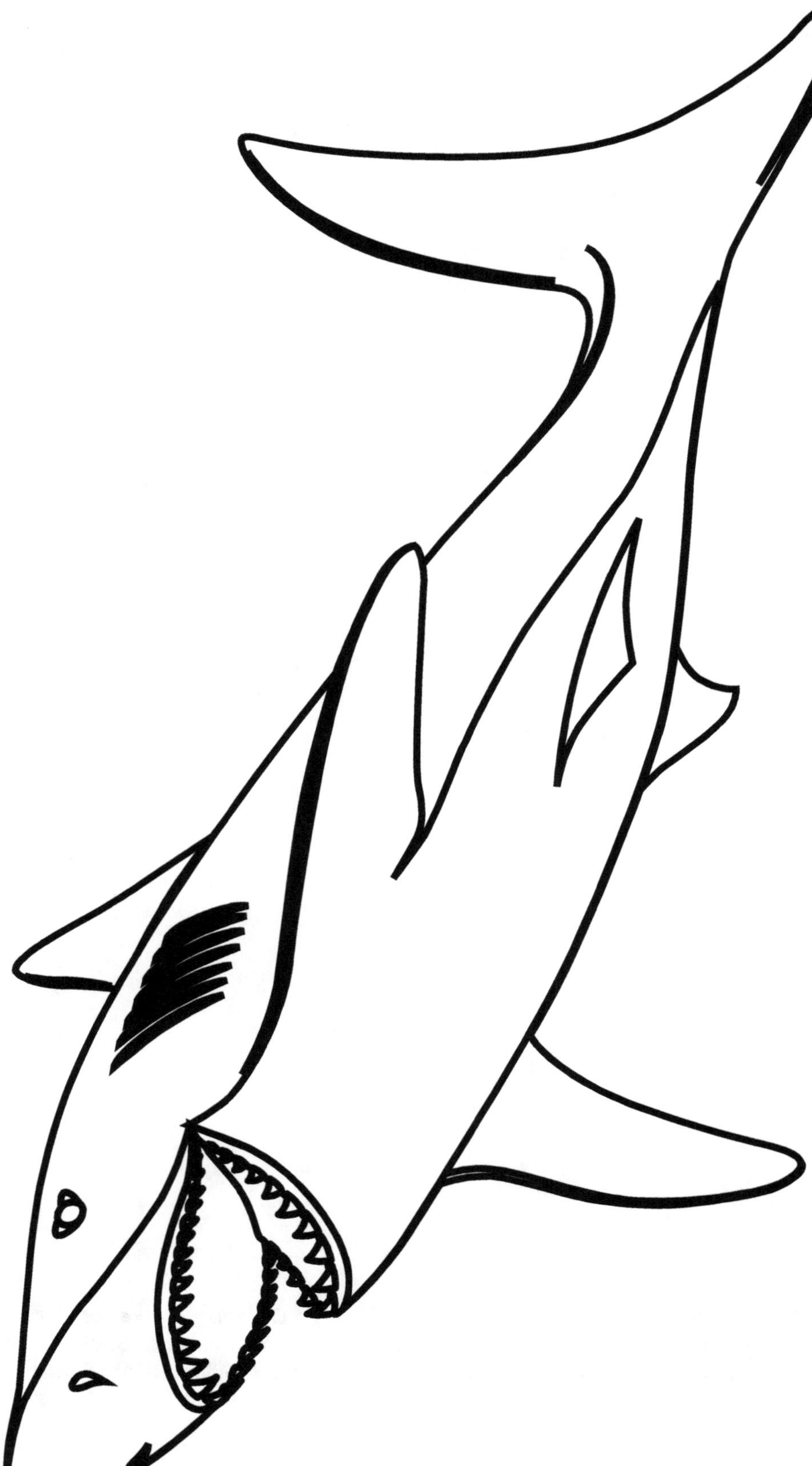

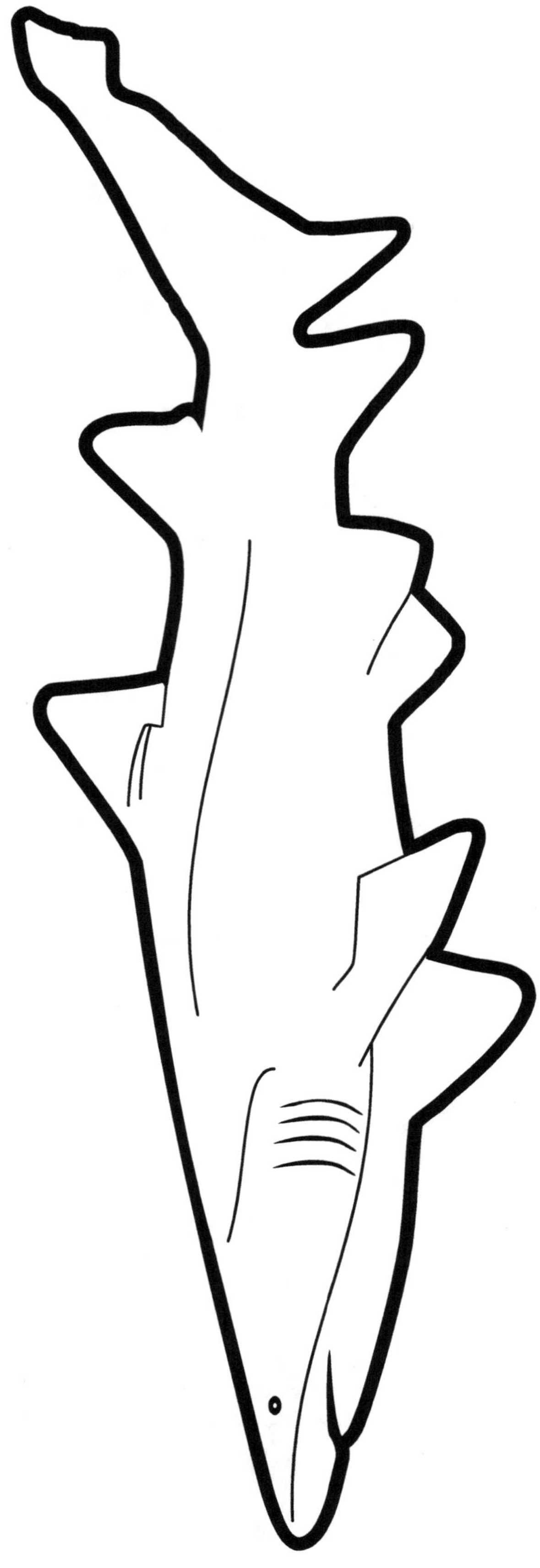

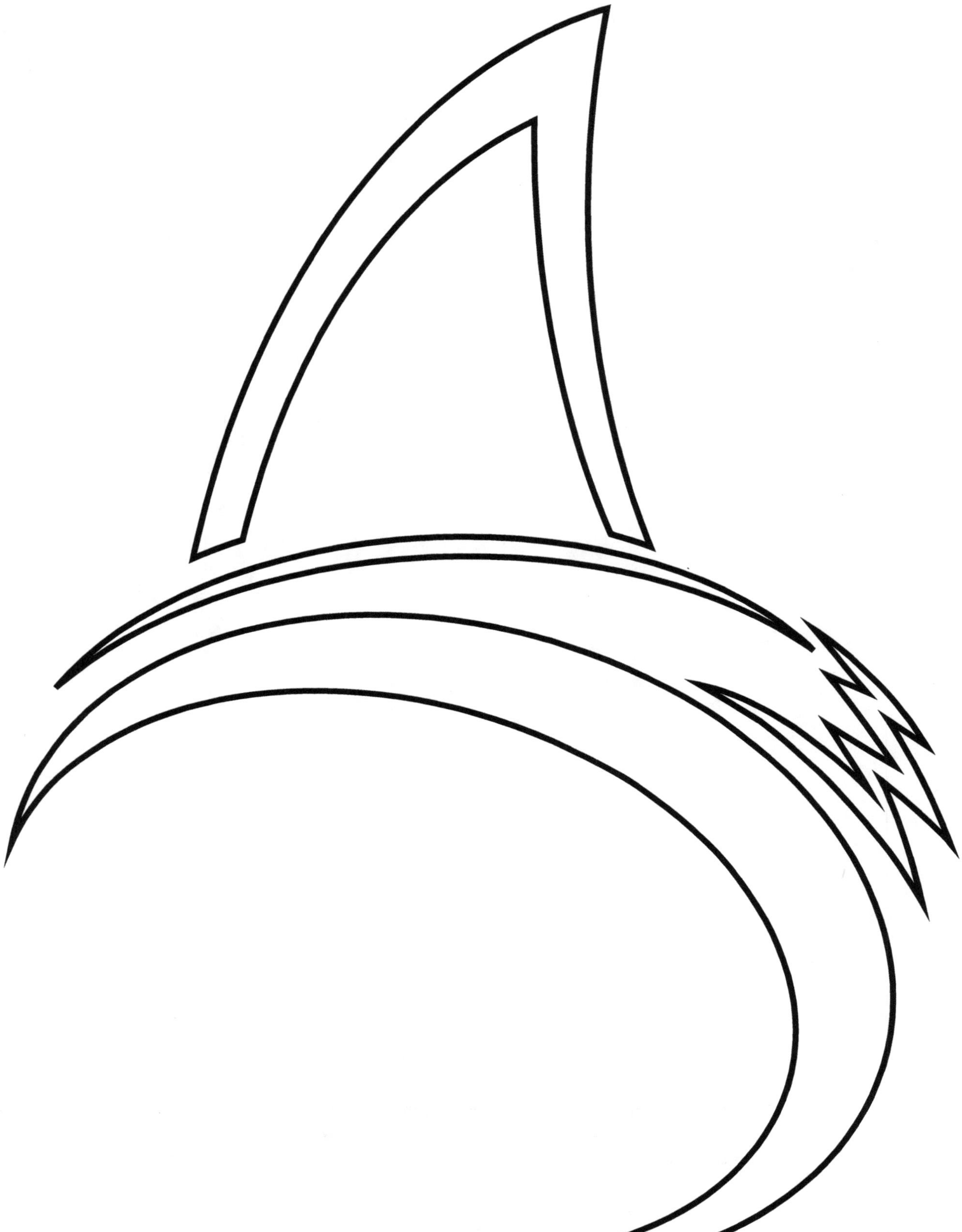

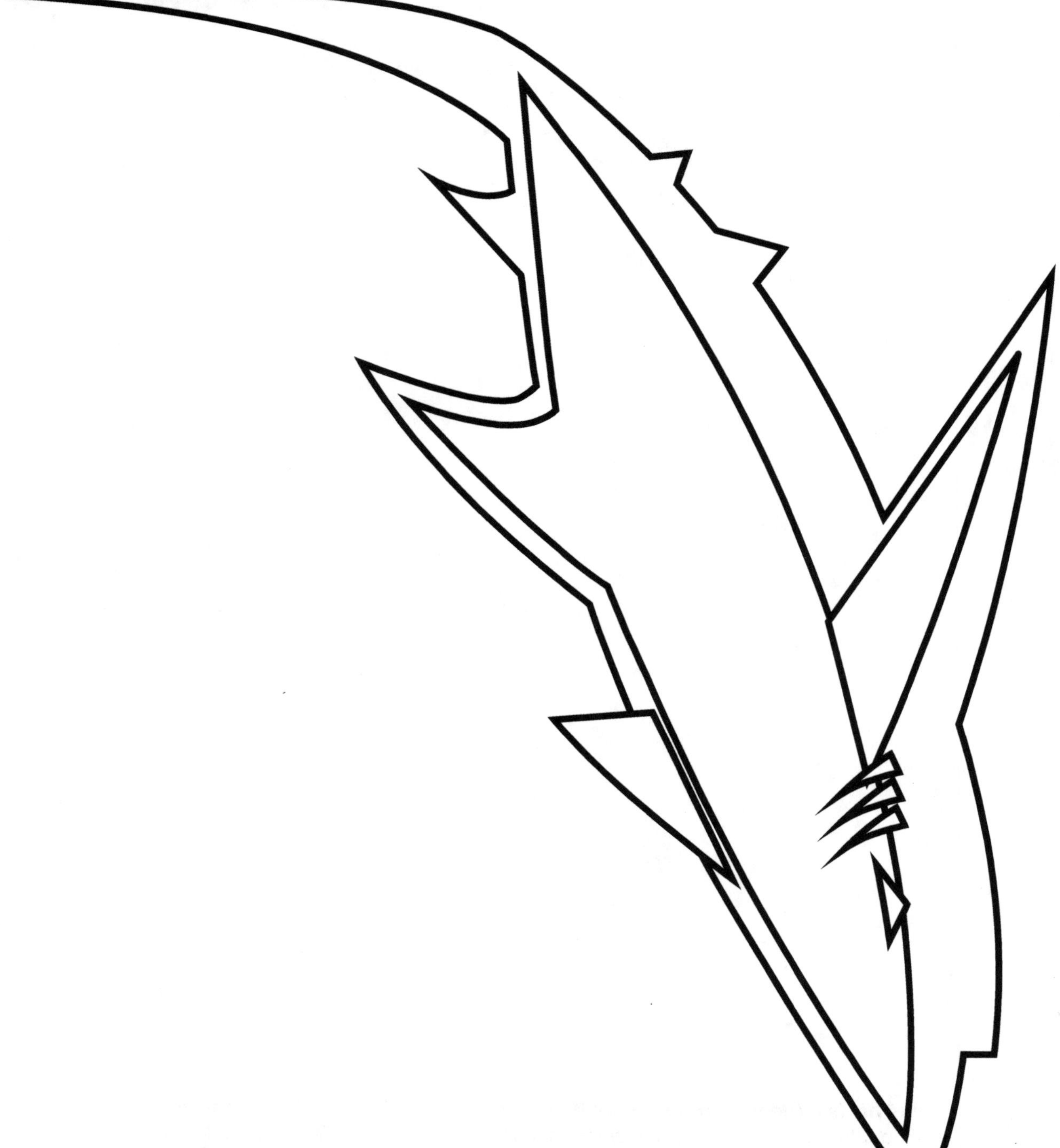

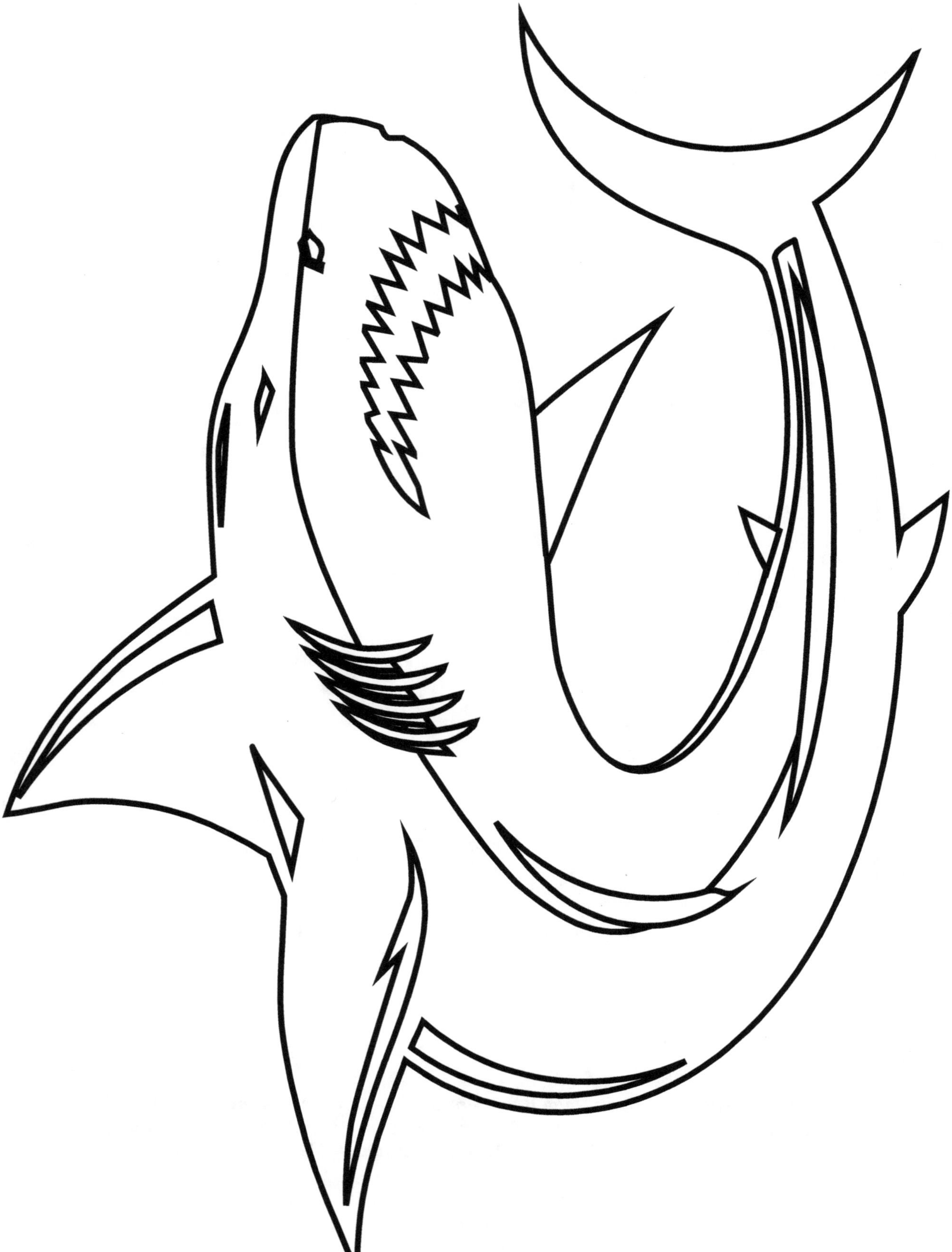

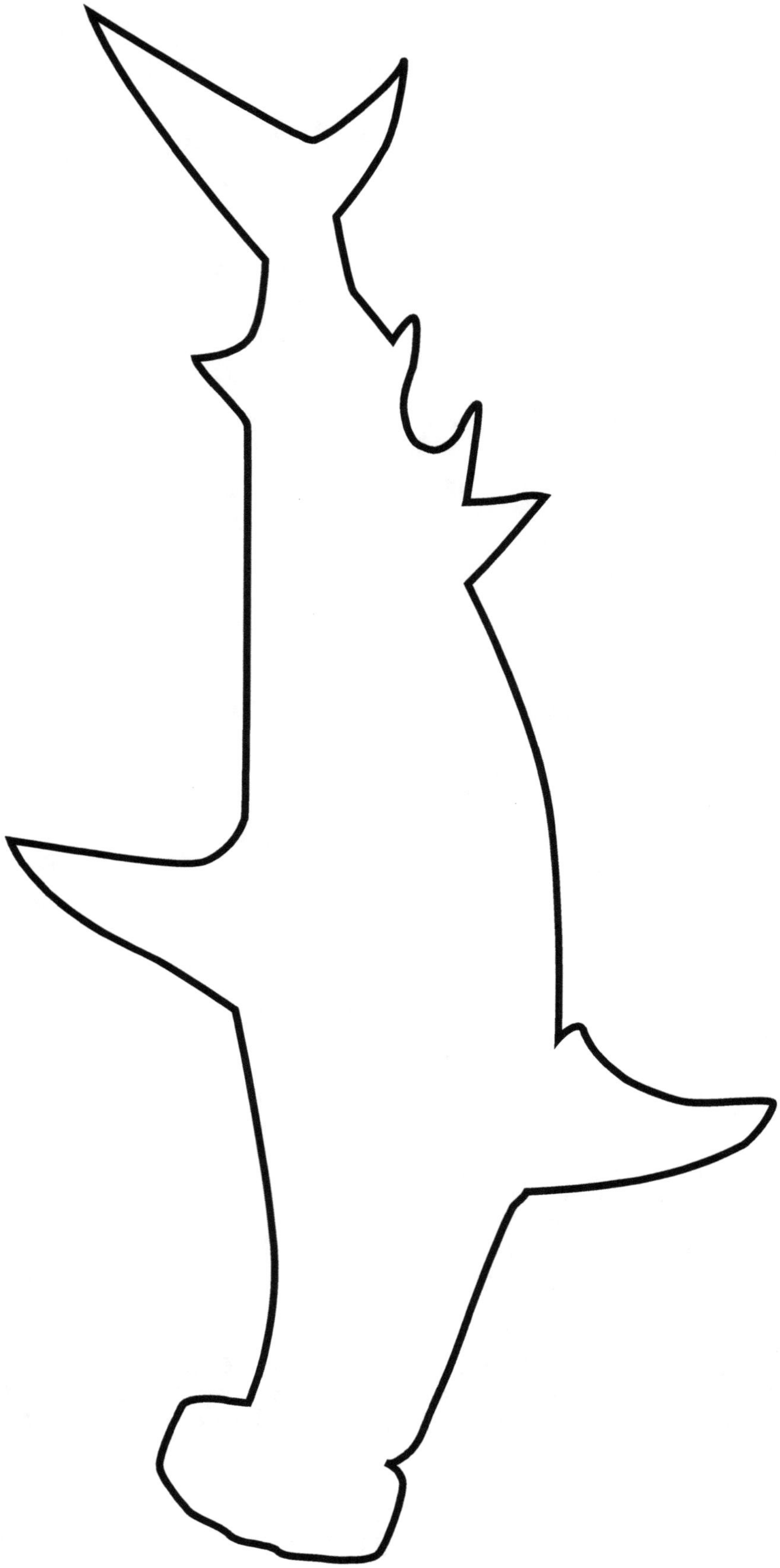

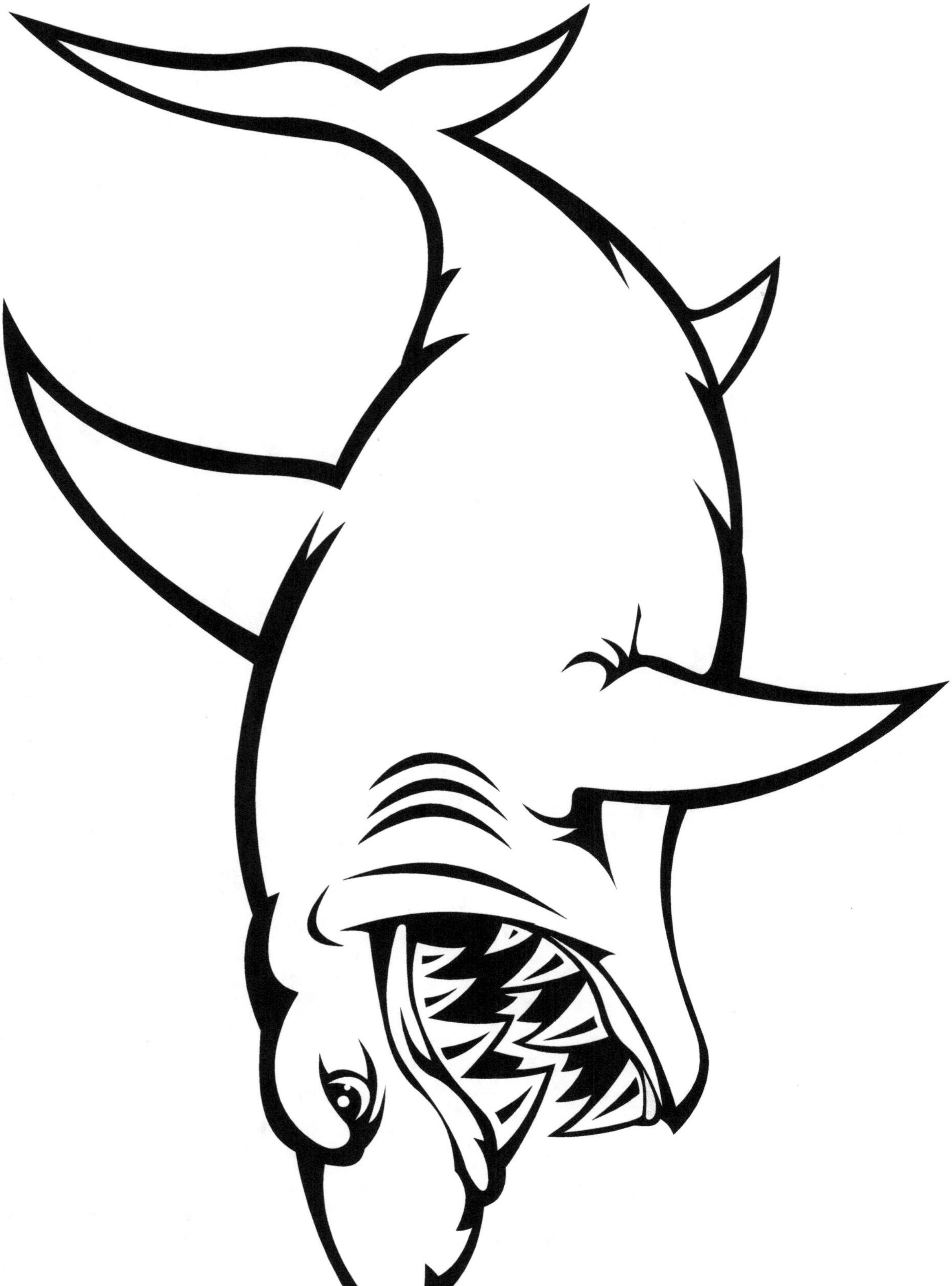

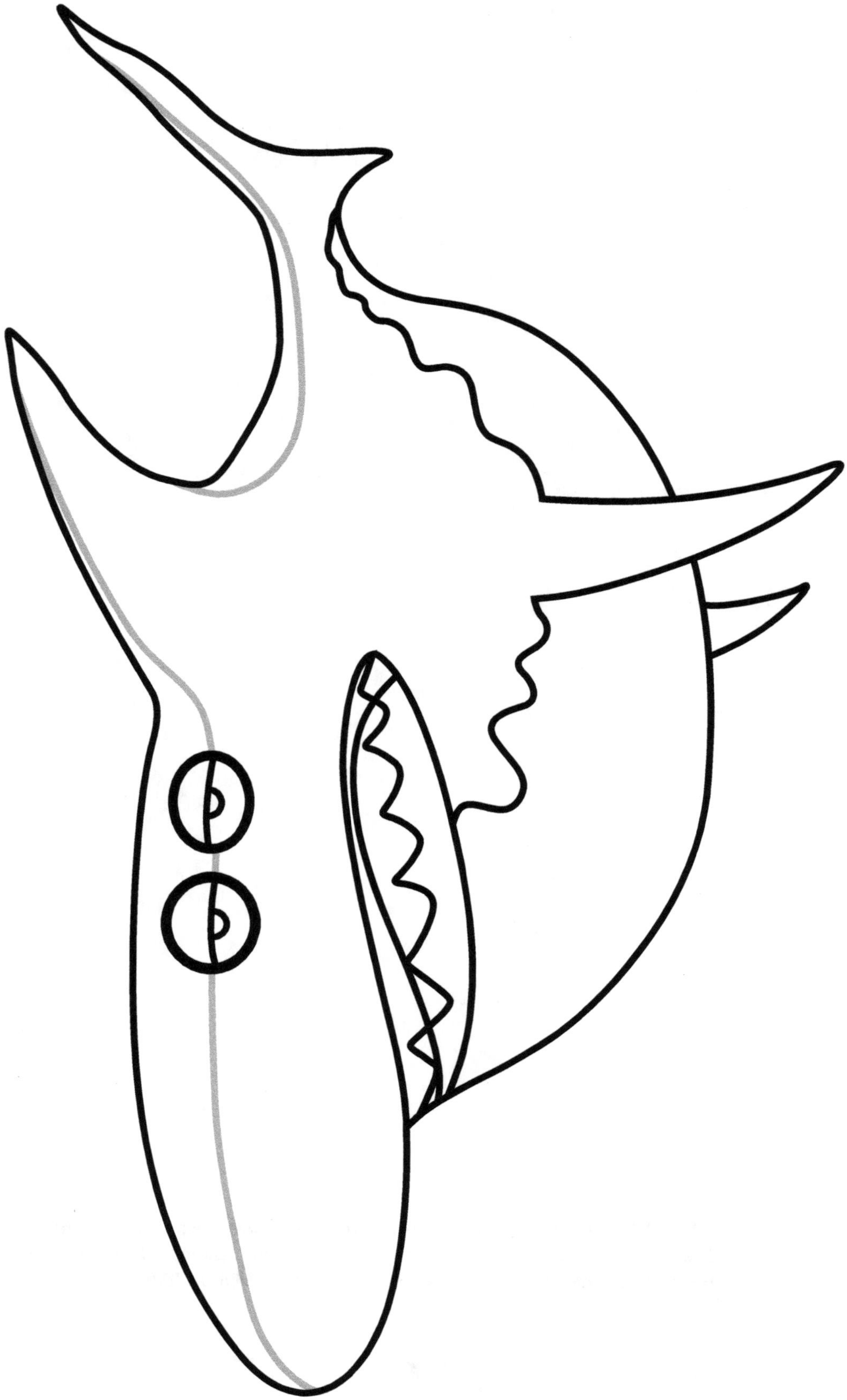

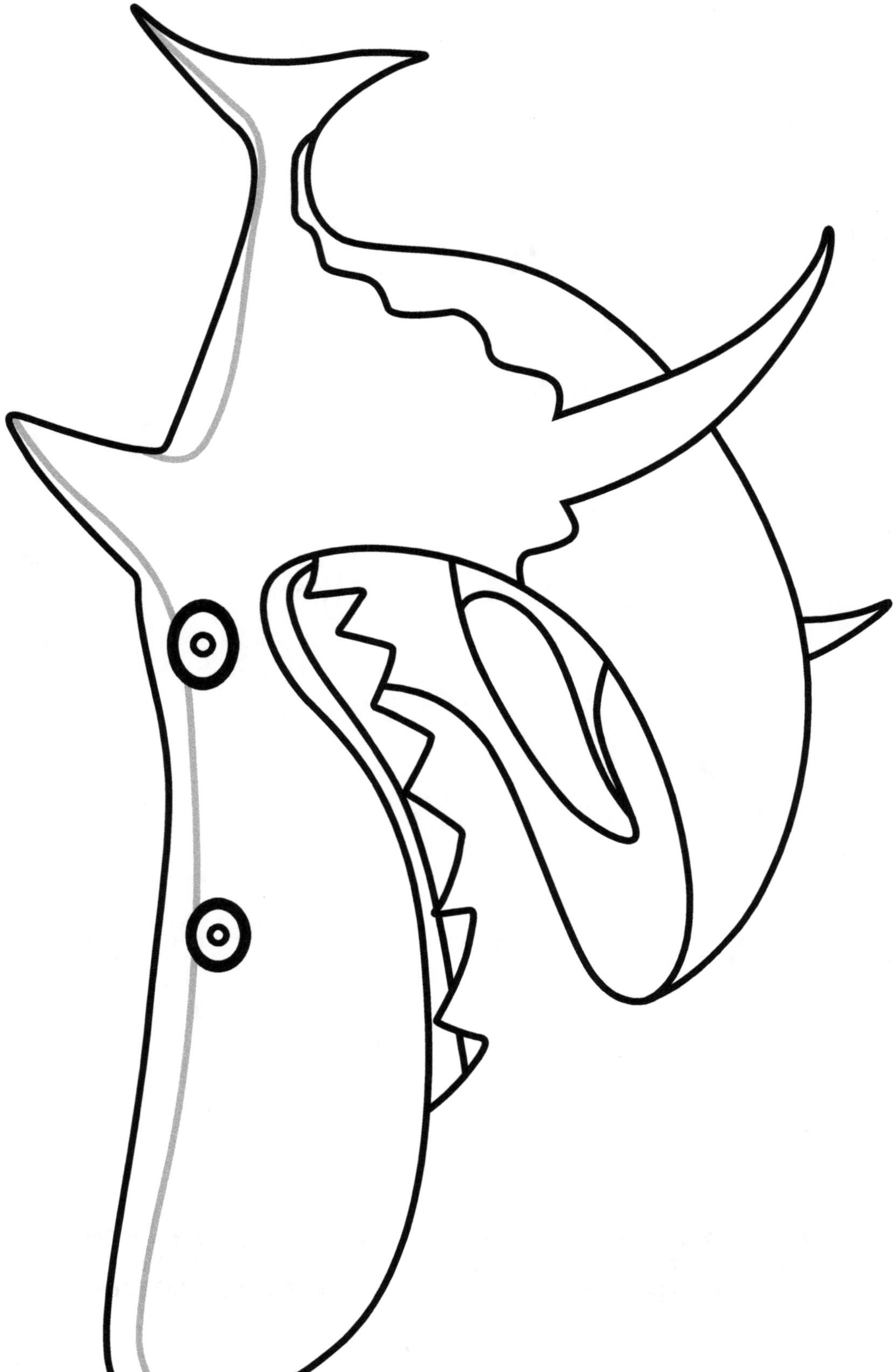

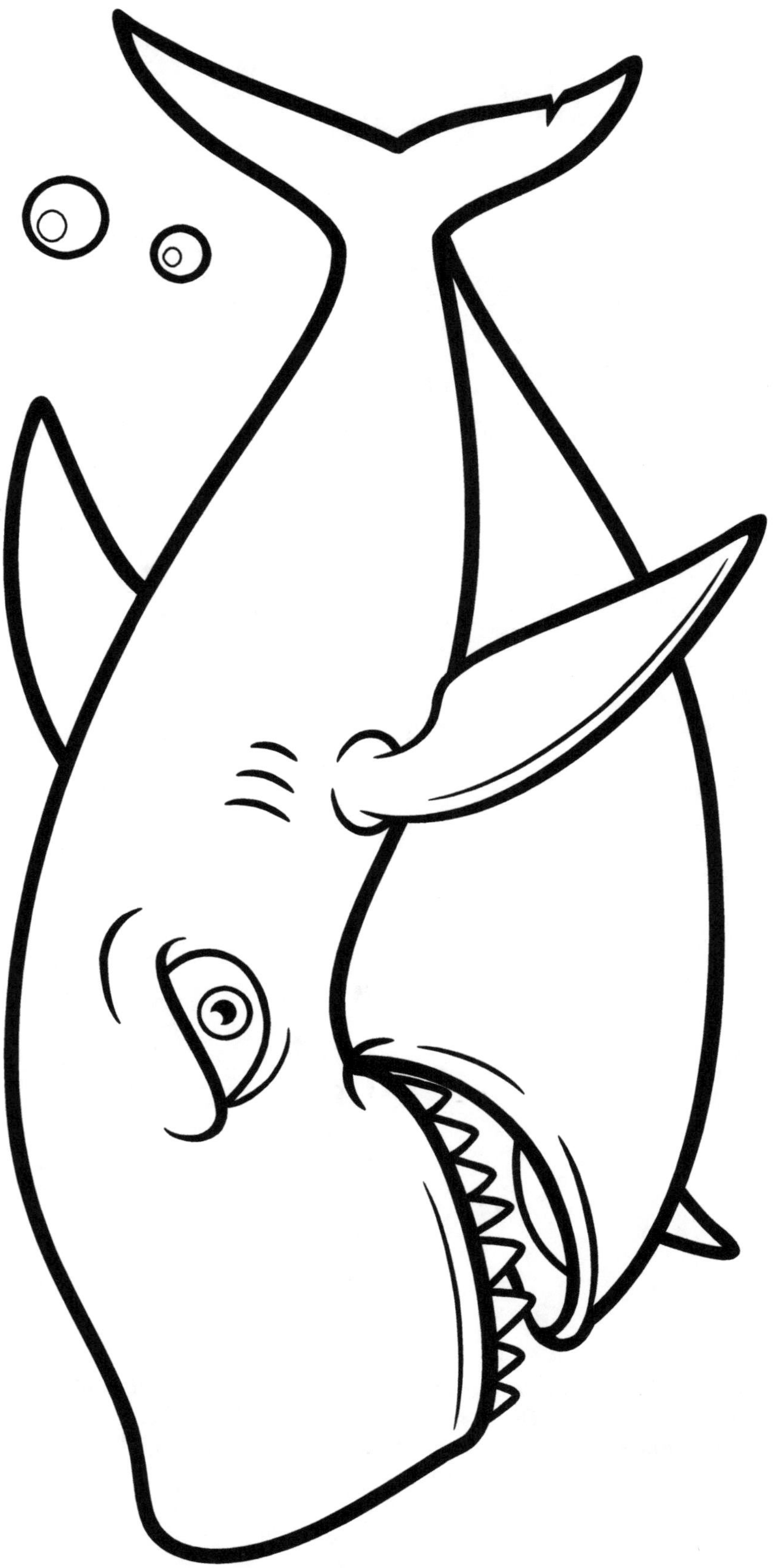

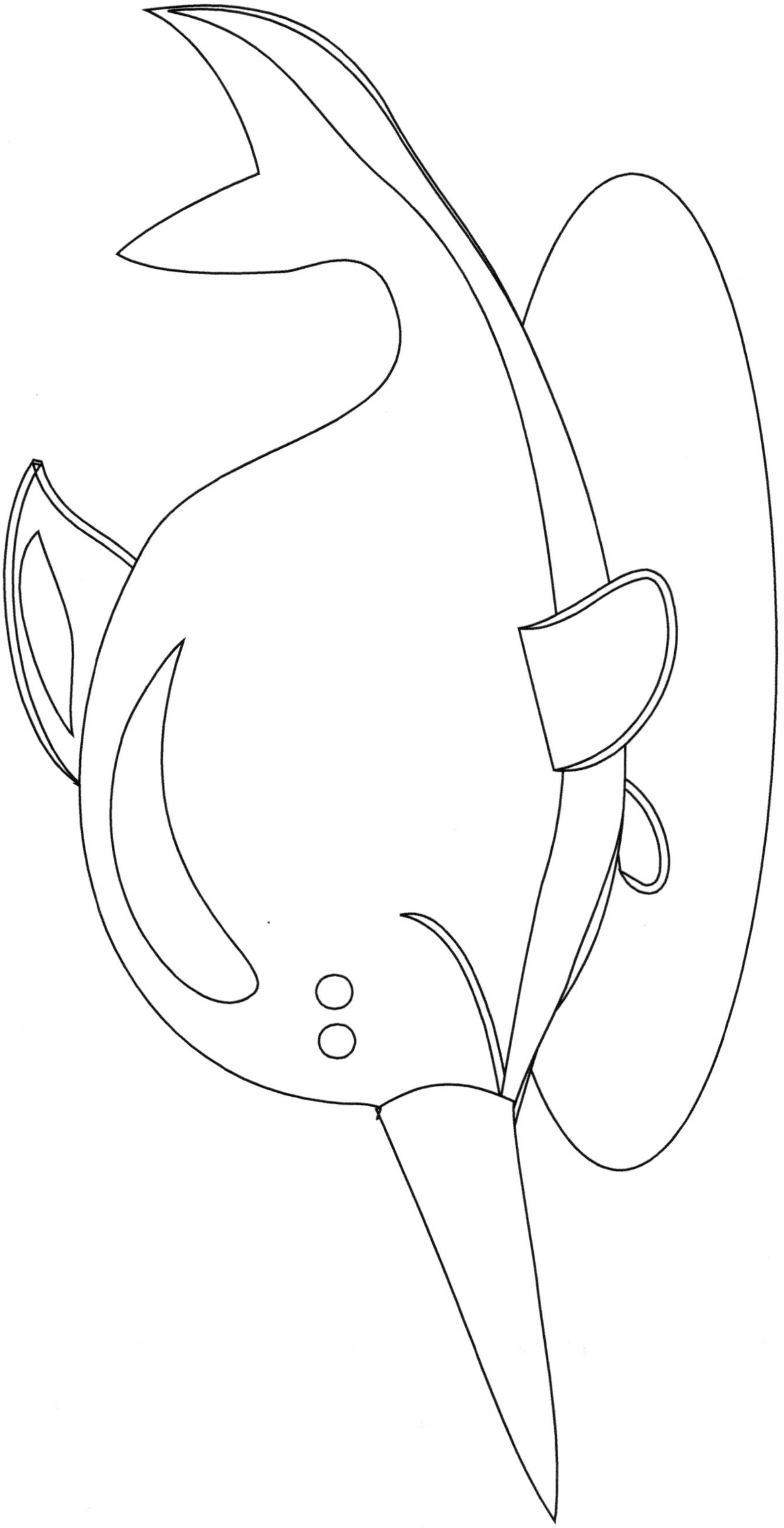

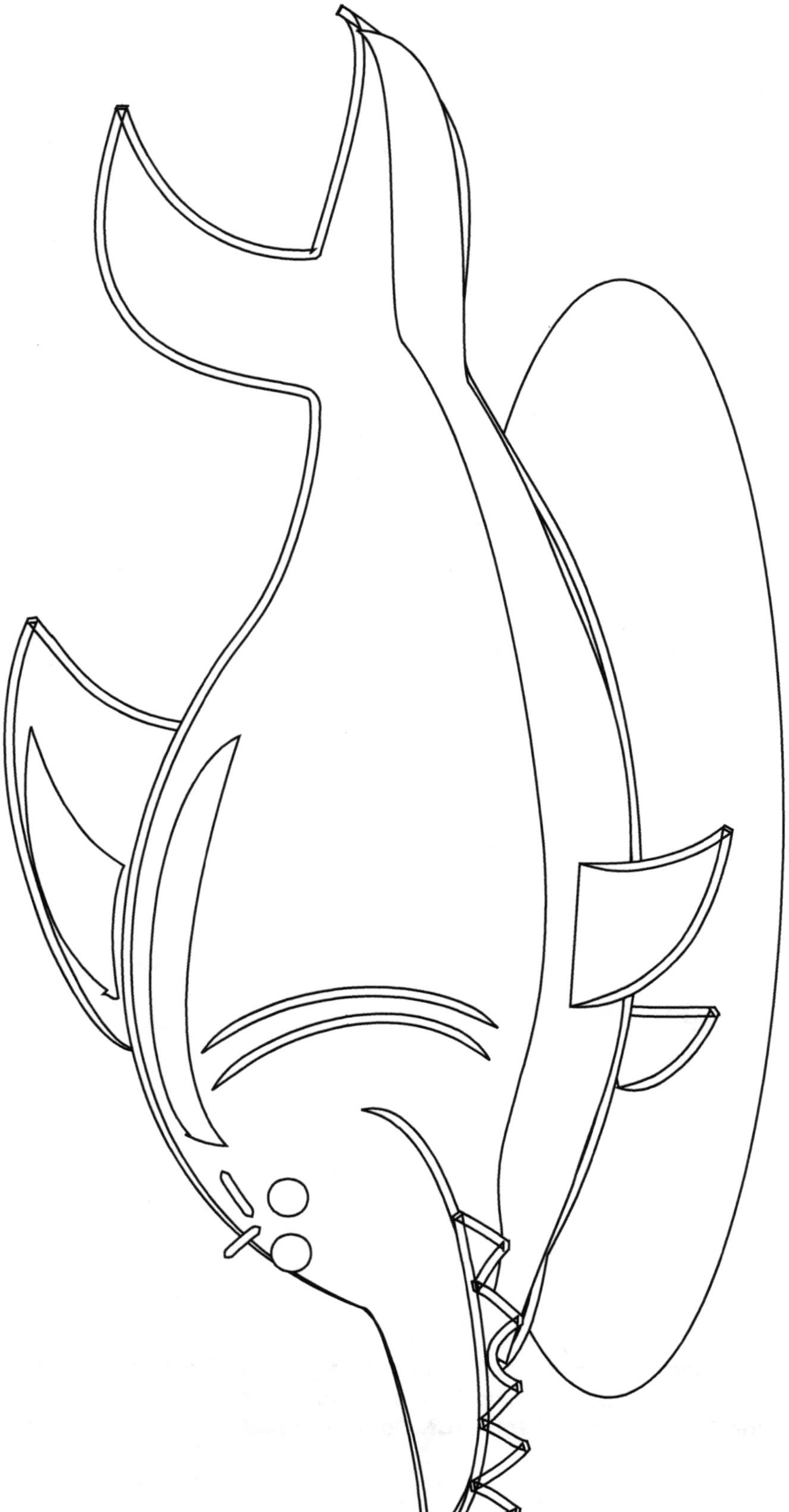

Printed in the USA
CPSIA information can be obtained
at www.ICGtesting.com
LVHW080344110224
771437LV00006B/515

9 781683 263326